The Friendly Dolphins

by
PATRICIA
LAUBER

SCHOLASTIC INC.
New York

ISBN 0-590-48134-7

12 11 10 9 8 7 6 5 4   5 6 7 8 9/9 0/0

Printed in the U.S.A.   23

First Scholastic printing, February 1995

The Friendly Dolphins

A small part of this book is based on an earlier book by Patricia Lauber, *The Friendly Dolphins* (Random House, 1963).

CONTENTS

The dolphin is the only creature who loves man for his own sake. Some land animals avoid man altogether, and the tame ones, such as dogs and horses, are tame because he feeds them. . . . The dolphin alone . . . has no need of any man, yet it is a genial friend to all and has helped many.

PLUTARCH, a writer of ancient Greece

A FRIEND
IN THE SEA

Once there was a boy named Dionysios, who lived long ago in Greece. He was much like any other boy. He lived with his family, went to school each morning, and played with his friends when school was out. We know about Dionysios for one reason only — a dolphin chose him as a friend. It happened this way.

On warm afternoons, Dionysios went to the beach. One day while he was swimming, a dolphin came up to him. At first Dionysios was frightened. The dolphin was much bigger than he was, and its mouth was full of sharp teeth. But he soon realized that the dolphin meant him no harm. It wanted to play. Losing his fear, Dionysios played with it.

The next day Dionysios went back to the beach. The dolphin was waiting for him. Again they played together. Day after day the dolphin was waiting for the boy, and the two became fast friends. Often the dolphin took Dionysios on its back. It carried him out to sea, then brought him safe to shore.

Word of what was happening spread far and wide. Crowds of people visited the beach to see the boy and his dolphin friend. The story was written down. And that is how we know about Dionysios, though he lived nearly 2,000 years ago.

Ancient writings are full of stories about dolphins. Here is one that took place near what is now Naples, Italy. The story tells of a dolphin that lived in a saltwater lake and of a poor boy who lived nearby. Every day the boy walked around the lake to reach his school. During these walks he became friends with the dolphin. He could call it, and it would come to be stroked. Soon each lost fear of the other.

One morning the boy stepped into the water and climbed on the dolphin's back. The dolphin carried him across the lake to school. After that the dolphin took the boy to school every morning and brought him home at night.

About the same time, there was a town called Hippo in North Africa. The boys of Hippo spent all their free time in the sea. One day a boy was swimming far out from shore when a dolphin joined him. It swam all around him. It dove under him, took him on its back, and rolled him into the sea. Then the dolphin again took the boy on its back. It carried him out to sea, turned, and carried him back to shore. The boy was safe, but frightened.

For several days the dolphin appeared when the boys went swimming. Each time the boys fled. Each time the dolphin seemed to invite them to stay. It leaped and dove in the way that dolphins play.

The men of Hippo came to watch the dolphin. After a while they began to feel ashamed. Why should anyone fear this friendly creature? They called to the dolphin. They went near it and touched it. The dolphin seemed to like being touched, and so they stroked it.

Now the boys became braver and swam near the dolphin. Among them was the boy who had first met the dolphin. He swam next to it. He climbed on its back and was taken for a ride. After that the boy and the dolphin often played together.

Many people came to see the friendly dolphin of Hippo, and this story, too, was written down.

It is clear that ancient Greeks and Romans knew many dolphins and liked them. We find dolphins on old coins, in wall paintings, and carved in gems. Most of all, we find them in poems, stories, and histories.

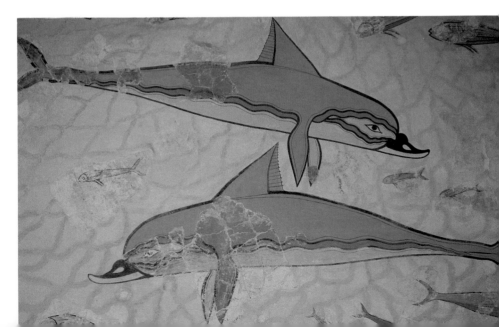

A dolphin appears on an ancient coin and in a painting on the wall of a Greek palace that is centuries old.

Some dolphin stories tell of things that could not have happened. But others tell how dolphins played around ships; how they helped fishermen by driving fish into their nets; how they saved the lives of people who were drowning. These stories are probably true, because the same things happen today.

Dolphins often accompany ships, sporting and racing around them. They ride the waves made by a ship's bow.

In some parts of the world, fishermen still depend on dolphins to drive fish into their nets. One of these places is a small town in Brazil. Here dolphins drive fish toward shore, trapping the fish between the beach and themselves. Then the dolphins take turns darting in and catching a fish to eat. When fishermen see the dolphins, they wade into the water. They cast their nets and catch the fish closest to shore. The dolphins do their fishing outside the nets. Men and dolphins have been fishing together on this beach since 1847.

Dolphins have also saved the lives of people who were drowning. One woman was caught in a strong current while swimming off a Florida beach. She had given up hope of breaking free when a dolphin gave her a great shove that landed her on shore. Perhaps this and other dolphin rescues were only dolphins at play, but even so, human lives were saved.

Do dolphins make friends with children? Were those ancient tales of boys and dolphins true? It seemed doubtful. No one had

Dolphins are often seen playing around boats and ships.

heard of such a thing taking place in modern times. Then, in 1955, it did happen. A wild dolphin made friends with another child.

This time it happened in New Zealand, near the town of Opononi. A dolphin came into the harbor and swam near the fishing boats. The fishermen found that she liked to be scratched with an oar. The dolphin, whom the men named Opo, grew bolder. She followed the boats in and began to play among the swimmers.

Opo was willing to play with grown-ups but preferred children. She chose to swim among them, making clear that she wanted to be petted. And Opo picked one child as her special friend, a 13-year-old girl named Jill Baker. If Jill swam off, Opo followed. Several times the dolphin swam between Jill's legs and gave her a short ride. She came to Jill for rubbing and petting. She even let Jill put small children on her back.

Like all dolphins, Opo loved to play. Someone gave her a colored beach ball. Opo soon invented a game with it. She tossed it into the air with her head, rushed to the place where it was going to fall, and tossed it again. Sometimes she tossed the ball into the air and batted it with her tail.

When people laughed or clapped, Opo seemed pleased. She leaped gaily out of the water.

As the year passed, more and more people came to see Opo. Sometimes as many as 1,500 came on a Saturday or Sunday.

Many dolphins allow themselves to be petted by children.

Then, in March 1956, Opo disappeared. When the fishermen found her, she was dead. Somehow she had become trapped in a rocky pool when the tide went out. All over New Zealand, people grieved for the friendly dolphin. She was buried at Opononi, and her grave was covered with flowers.

Many other dolphins have shown a liking for people. Free and wild, they choose to come near people and swim with them. They give every sign of liking human company. These dolphins are usually the kind named bottlenose dolphins, which live close to shore. They are also the ones you are likely to see in an oceanarium or marine park, and the ones this book is mostly about. It is easy to tell a bottlenose from other dolphins. Its mouth naturally curls up, and the bottlenose looks as if it were smiling.

The friendliness of bottlenose dolphins is one reason why many people like them. Another reason is that dolphins are interesting animals. For one thing, though they live in the sea, they are not fish. They are mammals, just as we are.

A BOTTLENOSE DOLPHIN'S BODY

tail flukes

back fin

blowhole

beak

flipper

ear

eye

Mammals
of the Sea

A dolphin swims by pumping its broad tail up and down. It steers mostly with twists of its tail. It uses its flippers to fine-tune the steering and also for balance and braking. The dolphin's streamlined body glides through the water at about 10 miles an hour.

Watch a dolphin swim and you will see that it does something that no fish does. It keeps coming to the surface. The curve of its back flashes into sight, then disappears as the dolphin dives. It swims underwater, then surfaces again.

Dolphins must surface to breathe. Fish can take oxygen out of water. Dolphins cannot. Like all mammals, they take oxygen from air.

A dolphin breathes through its blowhole, an opening in the top of the head. The blowhole opens when the dolphin surfaces and closes when it dives. During a dive, the dolphin holds its breath. Usually the dolphin breathes once or twice a minute,

**Unlike fish, dolphins must come
to the surface to breathe.**

while swimming near the surface. But it can hold its breath for as long as seven minutes when it needs to.

As a dolphin surfaces, it breathes quickly. It puffs out nearly all the used air in its lungs and fills them with fresh air. The cells of its body get a good supply of oxygen.

As cells use oxygen and food, they give off heat. Heat is carried to all parts of the body by the bloodstream. Like all mammals, a dolphin is warm-blooded; that is, it makes its own body heat.

Many animals do not make their own heat. They take their heat from the air or water around them. Their body temperature changes as the temperature outside them changes. In warm-blooded animals, body temperature always stays about the same. A dolphin's temperature is the same in cool water as in warm water.

To keep an even temperature, a mammal must give off heat, as well as make it. If no heat escaped, the body would become too hot. But mammals that live in cold air or water must also have a way of guarding body heat, of not giving off more heat than they can make.

Most mammals have a coat of fur that keeps out cold and holds in heat. Dolphins have no fur. Instead, dolphins and their relatives have a thick layer of fat, called blubber. The blubber is a covering that slows the escape of heat.

Dolphins have blubber instead of fur. Blubber gives the dolphin a stream-lined shape.

Blubber also fills out the body. It gives a dolphin a streamlined shape that slips easily through the water. If you touch a dolphin in cool water, you will notice that the outside of its body is cool. But its breath is warm. Inside its coat of blubber, the dolphin is always warm.

Dolphins have blubber in place of fur. But like all mammals, they breathe air and are warm-blooded. They also do something that only mammals do. In all the animal kingdom, only mammals nurse their young on milk. Dolphins nurse their young underwater — and they also give birth underwater.

The killer whale is a relative of the bottlenose dolphin.

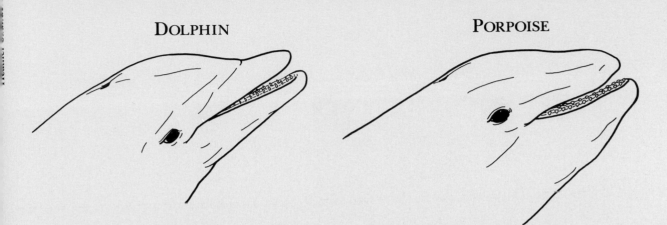

DOLPHIN

PORPOISE

DOLPHINS AND THEIR RELATIVES

Dolphins have many close relatives in the sea — the whales and porpoises. All belong to the same big group of mammals, and they are alike in many ways.

Dolphins and porpoises come close to being look-alikes, but there are differences. Most dolphins have jaws that are drawn out into a beak. A porpoise has no beak. Another difference is the shape of the teeth. A dolphin has cone-shaped teeth. A porpoise has spade-shaped teeth. Because these mammals are alike, many people call them all porpoises. (A second reason is that there is also a dolphin fish.) Other

people prefer to use both names, dolphins and porpoises.

To sort out whales, dolphins, and porpoises, scientists start by dividing them into two main groups. One group is made up of baleen whales. Instead of teeth, a baleen whale has what looks like a huge mustache in its upper jaw. It takes a big mouthful of water and food, then presses the water out through its mustache, or baleen. Food is trapped in the mouth. Most of the world's giant whales are baleen whales.

The second main group is made up of toothed whales. It has only one giant, the sperm whale. The rest are small whales, dolphins, and porpoises. There are about thirty kinds of dolphins.

15

bottlenose dolphin

SOME TOOTHED WHALES
sperm whale
bottlenose dolphin
pilot whale
killer whale
harbor porpoise
spotted dolphin
spinner dolphin

spinner dolphin

killer whale

gray whale

spotted dolphin

Marshall Peck

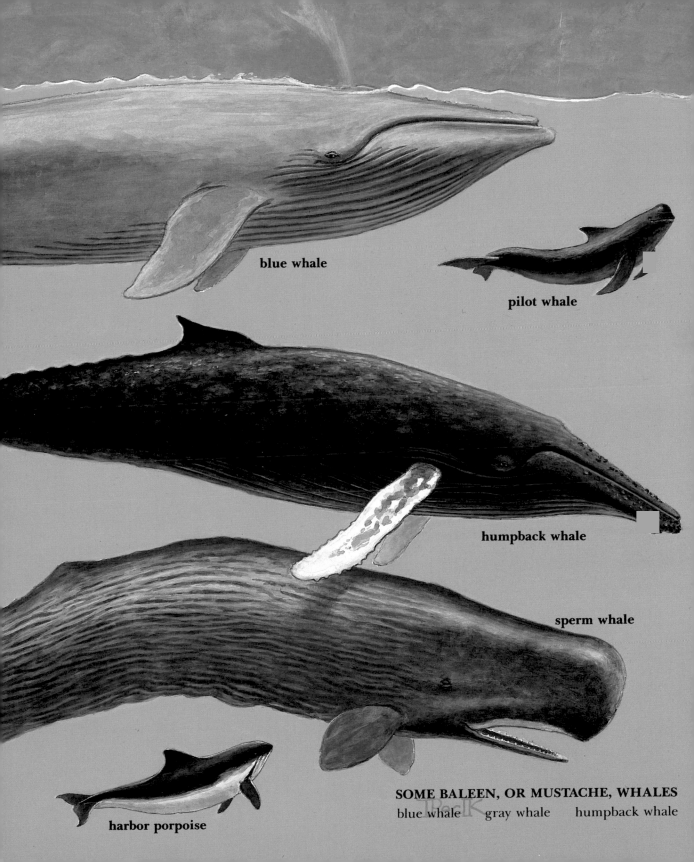

blue whale

pilot whale

humpback whale

sperm whale

harbor porpoise

SOME BALEEN, OR MUSTACHE, WHALES
blue whale   gray whale   humpback whale

MOTHERS AND YOUNG

Baby birds hatch out of eggs. So do most young fishes and snakes. But almost all baby mammals come into the world in a different way. They are carried inside their mothers' bodies until they are big enough to be born.

Some are born helpless. Kittens cannot see and cannot walk. Human babies cannot walk or take care of themselves in any way.

The young of horses and cows are different. Horses and cows are grazing animals that must move about to find food. Their young are born able to see and to travel beside their mothers.

Newborn dolphins are also able to see and to travel.

So far no one has seen the birth of a dolphin in the wild. But scientists have watched captive dolphins give birth. A birth may take anywhere from minutes to several hours.

Most baby mammals are born head first, but they are born on dry land. Their heads are in air, where they can breathe. A baby dolphin is born underwater. It would drown if it tried to breathe before it was free of its mother. A baby dolphin is born tail first.

Baby dolphins are born tail first.

19

As soon as the baby is free, it swims without help to the surface. There it takes its first breath of air.

The mother guides the baby, or calf, to her side. It travels close to her. The calf is lifted and supported by a kind of envelope of water created by the mother's movements. To keep up with her, it needs only to pump its tail from time to time.

A newborn dolphin looks like its mother, except that it is smaller. It is about four feet long, almost half the length of its mother. But it weighs only 30 pounds — its mother weighs 250 to 500 pounds. The skin has stripes and creases that show how the baby was curled up inside the mother. A newborn calf can see and hear well.

On its snout a baby has a few bristles, which soon fall out. These are the only fur, or hair, a dolphin ever has.

The calf first nurses when it is a few hours old. It nurses underwater for only seconds at a time. But it feeds often — ten to 20 times an hour. A nursing calf curls its tongue around its mother's nipple, forming a tube. When the mother tightens some muscles, she squirts milk through the tube, and the calf swallows.

The milk is rich, and a calf grows quickly. During its first year, it may gain 165 pounds and grow two feet in length. Young dolphins nurse for a year or longer, but they start to eat small fish before they are six months old.

A baby dolphin stays close to its mother.

Animals that live in water are hard to study in the wild. They are always on the move and usually out of sight. But for years at a time, some scientists have studied groups of bottlenose dolphins in the wild, swimming with them, watching them from boats, tracking them from land and from the air. Much of what we know comes from these studies.

The scientists see that dolphin mothers take good care of their young. A mother keeps her young calf at her side. As it grows older, she gives it more freedom but watches what the calf is doing. If she thinks it is in danger, she swims after it. When a calf sees its mother coming, it may start a game of catch-me-if-you-can. If the mother loses patience, she gives her calf a bite or holds it out of the water. After being punished, the calf swims with its mother for hours at a time. Sometimes the mother has help. A female without a calf may join her and help to care for the young dolphin.

When they are very young, calves nap a lot. Carried along beside their mothers, they close their eyes and sleep. From time to time, their tails pump and they surface to breathe. As they grow older, they sleep less. By the time they are a year old, they seem to think that sleep is a waste of playtime. Scientists have watched them play for as long as 30 hours without stopping.

Mothers and calves usually live in groups. The young play with one another and sometimes with adults. They chase each other, leaping and diving. They tease. One may offer another a fish, then snatch it away at the last moment. Two or three young are often in a kind of playground, an open space fenced in by their mothers' bodies.

The first year of life is the most dangerous for a young bottlenose. Some become ill and die during that time. Scientists are not sure what causes the deaths. But they suspect many can be traced to pollution, to poisonous wastes and chemicals dumped in the seas. A few deaths are caused by sharks. The mother of a dead calf is greatly upset. Perhaps thinking it is sick and in danger of drowning, she may hold it at the surface for days.

After five years, the young bottlenose is almost full grown and ready to live on its own.

If all goes well, though, a young dolphin swims with its mother for five years or more, until just before the birth of the next calf. By then the young bottlenose is almost full grown. It is catching and eating fish. It has learned how to live with other dolphins and how to recognize them. It has learned to know its home range. It is ready to take its place in the world.

THE WORLD OF
THE BOTTLENOSE

Bottlenose dolphins live in many parts of the world. But they are always near shore — in waters off open beaches, in inlets, bays, and waterways. Here they find the fish that are their food.

A dolphin catches a fish with its cone-shaped teeth. Usually the dolphin swallows the fish whole. But if the fish is too big, the dolphin may break it up by shaking it or rubbing it along the bottom. A full-grown dolphin eats ten to 20 pounds of fish a day. Nursing mothers must eat even more.

Dolphins hunt in several ways. Some hunt alone, taking whatever fish they meet. Off the west coast of Florida, dolphins have developed a special way of catching fish. A dolphin may whack a fish with its tail. The fish tumbles through the air for 20 or 30 feet, hits the water, and is stunned. The dolphin swims up and eats the fish.

Dolphins also work together to catch fish. A couple of dolphins may stir up the bottom with their beaks, disturbing the fish

A band of dolphins forms a circle. Sometimes they do this to catch fish.

that live there. As the fish flee, other dolphins catch them. Or dolphins may herd fish toward shore and take turns going in to feed on them. Sometimes a group of dolphins finds a school of fish. The dolphins circle the fish — around, above, and below — working them into a tight ball. Some dolphins feed on fish left out of the ball. Others swim into the ball to feed.

Dolphins that fish together seem to be dolphins that live together in bands. In studying them, scientists have found ways of telling one dolphin from another. They look for scars, nicks, or other markings that only one dolphin has. They give that bottlenose a name or number. Over the years they learn to recognize whole families — grandmothers, mothers, the young, and their older sisters and brothers. Grown males rarely live with these bands.

By day a band breaks up into small groups. Mothers with calves of the same age often swim together. Small groups meet, stay together for a while, then break up again.

When calves finally leave their mothers, they join wandering bands of other young dolphins and spend their days playing and sporting. But they feel close to their families. Daughters often visit their mothers' bands. The birth of a new calf brings visits from older brothers and sisters. Older sisters sometimes baby-sit a calf for their mothers.

Young males do not spend much time with their mothers' bands. They tend to stay by themselves. Each finds a male friend, most often one that grew up in the same band. The two — sometimes there are three — stay together for years, perhaps for the 40 to 50 years that a bottlenose may live. They fish together. They swim side by side, surfacing, diving, leaping. Each does exactly what the other does, at exactly the same moment.

As the males grow older, they travel from one band of females to another, looking for mates. Females are able to mate only once every four or five years. So far, scientists do not know how or

Male bottlenose dolphins pair up after leaving their mothers' bands.

why mates choose each other. But they have learned that sometimes males kidnap a female. This discovery was made by scientists studying bottlenose dolphins in waters off western Australia.

These scientists have seen that sometimes a pair of males is able to woo a female and get her to join them.

Another pair of males may then try to steal the female. Somehow, they persuade two more males to join them in a gang. The gang attacks and usually captures the female. Once that happens, the gang breaks up and the helpers swim off. But the next week, they may help another pair of males to steal the same female.

Males herd a female to keep her with them. Some females try to escape. Some are helped by female friends who attack the males. Sometimes the captured female does escape. But usually the males manage to keep her. When a calf is born, about a year after mating takes place, the males lose interest in the female and leave. The female may then join her mother's band and raise her calf there.

In the wild, a few bottlenoses appear to be loners, but most are not. They live and act with other dolphins — they are social animals. And they keep in touch with one another by sending out signals that sound to us like whistles and clicks.

**Dolphins are social animals.
They seldom live alone.**

WHISTLES AND CLICKS

The sea is a noisy place. Its waters are alive with noises made by fishes, crabs, shrimps, and other sea creatures. A person sitting in a boat does not hear these noises. But scientists have a way of listening in. Their chief tool is an underwater microphone, called a hydrophone. The sounds it picks up can be recorded on tape.

Dolphins are some of the noisiest sea dwellers. They are seldom quiet. They whistle; they clap their jaws together; they make noises that sound like squeaks, moans, mews, barks, creaks, and sputters.

A dolphin whistle is not like a human whistle. When you whistle, you pucker up your lips and blow through them. Dolphins don't use their lips, and usually they don't breathe out. Scientists are not sure how dolphins whistle, only that they do. They also know that a dolphin can whistle and make another kind of noise at the same time.

Dolphins use whistles and clicks and squawks to communicate.

31

While swimming underwater, dolphins are constantly sending out signals.

A whistle rises and falls, like a tune. It lasts only a second or two. To hear these whistles, scientists must slow down recordings of them.

The recordings show that every bottlenose has its own whistle. No two are the same. Each serves to identify the whistler. And that is how one dolphin recognizes another, just as you recognize a friend's voice on the telephone.

For the first few days after giving birth, a mother dolphin whistles almost constantly. That way the calf quickly learns its mother's sound. A baby dolphin can whistle on the day it is born. At first the whistle is a quavery sound, but in time a calf develops its own whistle. A mother and her calf whistle whenever they cannot see each other.

Dolphins are good at imitating sounds they hear. Sometimes one dolphin imitates the whistle of a friend or relative in greeting, much as you might call out a friend's name.

The way a bottlenose whistles tells something about the way it is feeling. A long series of loud whistles may show that a calf is lonely and wants to find its mother. A high whistle may show fear. If danger comes close, all whistling stops.

Other sounds have other meanings. A dolphin may snap its jaws together, making a loud, cracking sound. This is a threat.

A person playing ball with a captive dolphin is likely to tire of the game before the dolphin does. When the person stops playing, the dolphin shows it is not pleased. It lifts its head out of the water, makes a loud squawk, and slaps the water with its tail.

Scientists are not sure what other dolphin noises mean — all the moans, mews, barks, creaks, and squeaks. But they feel certain that the noises mean something to dolphins. A band of bottlenoses may laze about, sounding, one scientist says, "like an orchestra tuning up." After hours of this, they appear to reach a decision — they set out to go fishing, for example.

The noises do not seem to make a pattern. They do not seem to form a language. But they do seem to have meaning to bottlenoses.

When the noises are recorded and slowed down, scientists can hear that each noise is a burst of clicks.

Bottlenose dolphins also produce streams, or series, of clicks. To our ears, the clicks run together and sound like a door swinging on a rusty hinge. But recordings show that a dolphin may produce several hundred clicks a second. These clicks help the dolphin to find its way and to find food.

When a dolphin sends out a stream of clicks, the sounds travel through the water as far as several miles. When they hit solid objects, they echo back to the dolphin. Its brain sorts out the echoes. The dolphin learns about all the solid things that lie ahead. It knows where the things are, what shape they are, and how big they are.

A dolphin's eyes are set in the sides of its head. To see what is directly ahead, it must turn its head slightly and look with one eye. That is what this dolphin did as it leaped to take food from its trainer's hand. A dolphin has good eyesight.

That is how a dolphin can swim at top speed and never hit anything. It can find its way around rocks, ships, anchors, and docks. It can find its way on the blackest of nights and in muddy or cloudy water.

Bottlenose dolphins have good eyesight, both underwater and above water. But the echoing clicks tell them far more than the sharpest eyes can see.

Dolphins are not the only animals that send out sounds and use the echoes to find their way. Sperm whales do it. Shrews do it. So do bats. In fact, the first studies of this ability were made in bats. Scientists found that bats were using echoes to locate what was ahead of them. So the ability was named echolocation.

Humans also make use of echolocation. A blind person tapping a stick is using it. Two electronic instruments use it, too. One is radar, which sends out radio waves and records their echoes. The other is sonar, which sends out sound waves. Sonar is used underwater, where radar does not work. Dolphin sonar is far better than anything humans have invented. Electronic sonar cannot tell a wooden ship from one made of steel. Tests with captive dolphins show they can tell aluminum from iron or copper. A captive dolphin, which has been blindfolded with soft rubber cups over its eyes, can find a three-inch metal ball that is 370 feet away. The distance is longer than the length of a football field. Dolphins' sensing of echoes is called either sonar or echolocation.

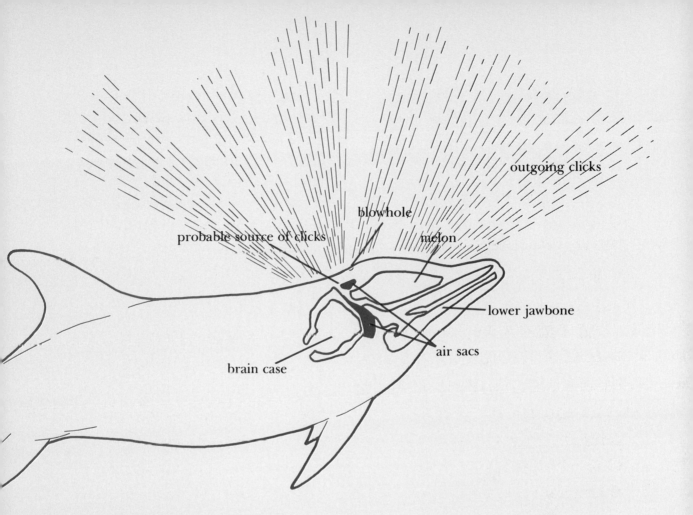

probable source of clicks

blowhole

melon

outgoing clicks

lower jawbone

air sacs

brain case

DOLPHIN ECHOLOCATION

Scientists are not sure how dolphins make and send out their clicks. But many think the clicks are produced in an area just below the blowhole, which vibrates like the lips of a trumpet player. The brain case and air sacs act like a mirror, bouncing the stream of clicks forward. A fatty region, called the melon, helps to direct the clicks. Returning echoes are received in the lower jawbone. They travel along a channel of oil to the inner ear. The dolphin's brain makes sense of the signals from the ear.

DOLPHINS IN DANGER

In warm waters of the eastern Pacific, yellowfin tuna often swim beneath dolphins. When fishermen trap the tuna with huge nets, they also trap the dolphins. The dolphins, mostly spotted and spinner dolphins, drown. Tens of thousands of dolphins have died in tuna nets.

The United States has passed laws to help protect the dolphins. Other countries have agreed to make sure fewer dolphins are killed. But still many die.

Scientists are trying to help the dolphins. They want to find out why tuna and dolphins swim together. They want to learn when dolphins and tuna separate, when tuna can be caught without harming dolphins. They want to study dolphin echolocation and fishing nets. Perhaps there is a way to help dolphins escape nets.

You can help, too. If your family buys canned tuna, make sure the label says "dolphin-safe." Make sure fresh tuna was "caught on long lines." When tuna is caught on long lines, no dolphins are harmed.

Bottlenose dolphins use echolocation to find fish. They may also use sound to stun fish. Tape recordings have been made of wild dolphins while they were feeding. The tapes recorded trills of clicks followed by much lower, louder banging noises. The noises sounded like exploding hand grenades. Bottlenose dolphins do not always make banging noises when feeding. But the noises are hard to explain unless they are used to stun prey.

Captive dolphins do not make banging noises. Scientists think dolphins themselves might be stunned or hurt by echoes from the tank walls. Dolphins do, however, use echolocation in their tanks every few seconds. They are aware of everything that happens. In one test, a teaspoon of water was splashed into a tank. The dolphins began to click. When they found nothing, they stopped.

Much of what we know about dolphin sonar has been learned from captive dolphins.

Captive dolphins have taught us much about dolphin intelligence.

PLAY AND INTELLIGENCE

At oceanariums, bottlenose dolphins leap, twist, and spin. They jump through hoops. They shoot baskets. They soar out of the water, grasp a rope, and ring a dinner bell. Most captive dolphins do tricks they have been taught by human trainers. But some dolphins learn tricks just by watching other dolphins do them. Bottlenoses are good at learning and also at inventing ways to amuse themselves.

Some dolphins have invented a baseball game. One dolphin pitches, throwing a ball toward the bat of a human hitter. Other dolphins field the ball. They try to get it back to the pitcher before the batter can reach base.

Young dolphins enjoy teasing other animals that live in their tank. One took to teasing a fish. The fish was trying to swim forward. The dolphin kept taking it by the tail and pulling it backward. Each time, the dolphin let the fish go. The fish hurried away. Then the dolphin again grasped its tail and pulled it backward.

A captive dolphin in Hawaii jumps over a canoe. Dolphins are good at learning tricks.

Another dolphin enjoyed teasing a large fish that lived in a cave of rocks. The dolphin would lay a piece of squid at the mouth of the cave, back off, and wait. Each time the fish came out to eat the squid, the dolphin snatched the squid away.

Dolphin games are fun for the dolphins. They are fun for the people who watch. And they are of interest to scientists, because the games tell something about dolphin intelligence. They seem to show that dolphins are among the most intelligent mammals.

Animal intelligence is never easy to measure. And it is very hard to measure in an animal that lives in water. Scientists cannot use the same tests that they use for land animals. But dolphin behavior offers many clues.

For example, teasing is a sign of intelligence in animals.

Teasing is action taken on purpose. Teasers expect something to happen because of their actions. That is, they think ahead.

Dolphins think ahead in other ways, too. At one oceanarium, dolphins were taught to pick up litter that had blown into their tank and take it to their trainer. For each piece of litter, a dolphin was given a reward — a snack of fish. One dolphin seemed to be finding more litter than any of the others. The trainer discovered that this dolphin had hidden several paper bags under a platform. Instead of delivering a whole bag to the trainer, the dolphin was tearing off a piece, bringing that, and getting a reward. Then it went back and tore off another piece.

Curious dolphins greet visitors at the oceanarium.

Dolphins can invent games, make up rules, and later change the rules. They learn games from one another.

These abilities are signs of high intelligence. Another sign is the ability to solve problems.

Two scientists saw a pair of bottlenoses teasing an eel. The eel was in a crack in a rock, and the dolphins were trying to pull it out. They could get at the eel. They could pull it back and forth between them. But they could not get it out. After a while, one bottlenose swam off. It came back with a newly killed scorpion fish. It used the sharp spines of the fish to poke the eel. The eel popped out of the crack. The dolphins caught it, took it to the middle of their tank, and let it go. Scientists never pretend to know what an animal is thinking. But this looked like good problem solving.

Three dolphins had been taught to swim together and to jump out of the water at the same time. At the end of their act, each was given a fish. After several weeks, one of the three began to lag behind. Because the dolphins were supposed to be a team, no reward was given. The same thing happened again and again. Finally, one of the two dolphins turned on the lagger and bit him several times on the head. After that the third dolphin kept up and all were given their rewards.

Teasing and problem solving are two signs of dolphin intelligence. Are dolphins smart enough to learn and remember a

Akeakamai was trained to understand sign language.

language? One scientist, working in Hawaii, decided to find out. He invented two languages and rules for using them. Then he set about teaching and testing two bottlenose dolphins named Phoenix and Akeakamai (say AH-KEY-AH-KAY-MY).

Phoenix was taught a language that she heard. The words in this language were underwater sounds made by a computer.

Akeakamai was taught a language that she saw. The words in this language were signs, or gestures, that trainers made with their arms and hands.

Both dolphins learned their languages. They learned to match names with objects in their pool. They learned to match words with actions — with things they could do. They also learned the rules of their languages.

If, for example, a dolphin was told "Frisbee fetch hoop," she took the Frisbee to the hoop. If she was told "Hoop fetch Frisbee," she took the hoop to the Frisbee.

Akeakamai worked with several trainers. No two made gestures quite the same way. Yet the dolphin understood all of them. Told "Ball over," she would jump over the ball in her pool. She also understood something much harder. She knew that "ball" meant more than just the ball in her pool. It could mean any kind of ball — big or small, soft or hard, in the pool or out

of the pool. When the trainer showed her a ball and then made the sign for "over," the dolphin jumped over the ball in her pool.

Phoenix knew the words for "hoop" and for "through." When she heard the words, she would swim through a hoop floating at the surface. Then she learned a word for "bottom," meaning something lying on the bottom of the pool. Told to swim through a hoop on the bottom, Phoenix dived and stuck her beak under the hoop. Once the hoop was upright, she swam through it. She had understood what she was told — and she had also solved a problem.

Akeakamai was taught to answer simple questions. For example, "Ball question" meant, "Is there a ball in the tank?" To answer "Yes," she pushed one of two paddles in her tank. To answer "No," she pushed the other paddle. This test showed that she understood "ball" even when there was no ball to be seen.

Both dolphins were able to understand a language. That is a sign of intelligence. But it does not mean that dolphins have a language of their own. It does not mean that they talk among themselves. It would be wonderful if they did, because we could learn the language and talk with them. But so far there is no reason to think that dolphins talk.

Still, one thing we know for sure is that we have much more to learn about — and from — these friendly mammals of the sea.

Dolphins can learn to match names with objects.

INDEX

ABOUT THE AUTHOR

Patricia Lauber has written more than 90 books for young readers. Most of them are science books. In addition to dolphins, she has written about dinosaurs, whales, earthworms, and trees. She has written about planets, seeds, octopusses, and earthquakes — and other subjects that children like to read about.

Many of Ms. Lauber's books have won awards. *Volcano: The Eruption and Healing of Mount St. Helens* was a Newbery Honor Book (1987). This book, as well as three others — *Tales Mummies Tell, The News about Dinosaurs,* and *From Flower to Flower: Animals and Pollination* — were honored by the New York Academy of Sciences.

Ms. Lauber has earned several awards for her writing, including the Lifetime Achievement Commendation from the 1992 National Forum on Children's Science Books at Carnegie Mellon University and the 1988 Eva L. Gordon Award from The American Nature Society.

Ms. Lauber is married and lives with her husband in Connecticut.